LIBERIA PRESIDENTS
1847-2021

Ophelia S. Lewis

VILLAGE TALES PUBLISHING

MINNEAPOLIS, MINNESOTA

Copyright © 2021 Ophelia S. Lewis

All rights reserved. No part of this publication may be reproduced, stored in a retrieval system, or transmitted in any form or by any means, electronic, mechanical, photocopying, recording or otherwise, without prior written permission of the copyright owner. Published in the Untied States by Village Tales Publishing.

We make no copyright claim on any statistical data on any page within this book, nor on any non-original graphics, and/or pictures not produced by Village Tales Publishing.

Certain statistical data is gathered from numerous public domain reference materials, and every effort is made to be as accurate as possible when disseminating information on any worldwide destination or subject. We are not responsible for unintentional data entry errors or omissions.

All the information provided in this book is strictly for entertainment purposes only. Although the author and publisher have made every effort to ensure that the information in this book was correct at press time, the author and publisher do not assume and hereby disclaim any liability to any party for any loss, damage, or disruption caused by errors or omissions, whether such errors or omissions result from negligence, accident, or any other cause.

A catalog record for this book is available from the Library of Congress

Library of Congress Control Number: 2021908992

ISBN: 9781945408694

First published in the United States in 2021

Interior & Cover Designed by OASS

Village Tales Publishing provides traditional publishing services and turnkey services to individuals that seek to successfully self-publish and promote their books. We handle all aspects of publishing; editing, cover design, production, marketing and order fulfillment.

Please visit our websites:

www.villagetalespublishing.com

www.oass.villagetalespublishing.com

Printed in the United States of America

Contents

Author's Note 4
The President of Liberia 5
Office of the President 6
Joseph Jenkins Roberts 7
Stephen Allen Benson 8
Daniel Bashiel Warner 9
James Spriggs Payne 10
Edward James Roye 11
James Skivring Smith 12
Anthony W. Gardner 13
Alfred F. Russell 14
Hilary R. W. Johnson 15
Joseph J. Cheeseman 16
William D. Coleman 17
Garretson W. Gibson 18
Arthur Barclay 19
Daniel E. Howard 20
Charles D. B. King 21
Edwin J. Barclay 22
William V. S. Tubman 23
William R. Tolbert 24
Samuel K. Doe 25
Interim Leaders I 26
Amos Sawyer 26
David Kpomakpor 26
Wilton G. S. Sankawulo 27
Ruth Perry 27
Charles Taylor 28
Interim Leaders II 29
Moses Blah 29
Gyude Bryant 29
Ellen Johnson Sirleaf 30
George Weah 31
Brigs & Ships 32
Liberia Presidents Crossword Puzzle 33
The Declaration of Independence 34
The Lone Star Forever 35
Bibliography 36
Answers 37
Ophelia S. Lewis 38

Author's Note

Since 1847, our Commanders-in-Chief have led Liberia through every challenge. In this book, you will get to know all the presidents. Organized chronologically by president, each entry covers the significant accomplishments and events of the presidential term; cabinet members, election results, groundbreaking legislation, and careers before the presidency. Fast facts, from Joseph Jenkins Roberts to George Weah, will help identify each president's birthplace, achievements, events, triumphs, and legacies. Famous and lesser-known presidents are also included. Also, learn about the Declaration of Independence and other historical events. Throughout the book, footnotes are added on every page to help students with unfamiliar words.

There are even word games in the book. The puzzles included have a separate list of clues. These are the words to look for. Circle each word in the diagram, then cross them off the list. Remember, words run not only vertically, horizontally, and diagonally but could be spelled backward as well. Accents are not included in the puzzle diagram, nor are spaces between words. If you get stuck, the answers are included at the back of the book, beginning on page 37.

The Liberia Presidents book is a helpful learning tool for elementary school students and provides a good reference tool for anyone. To learn more about Liberia, use the bibliography list I used in my research. Even better, visit the online library, www.library.liberialiterarysociety.org, explore books written by Liberian authors and non-Liberian authors. Buy the books. Read the books. Review the books. We must preserve Liberia's literary works.

I hope you enjoy this book as much as I did writing it. There are other Clever Children Gamebooks I think you will enjoy. I created the series as a way to make learning fun. You can find all my books on my website at www.ophelialewis.com. Connect with me on social media, @ophie2020.

Have fun learning!

The President of Liberia

To be president of Liberia you must:

- Be a natural born citizen of Liberia; (only a black person can be a citizen)
- Be at least thirty-five years old;
- Own real property valued at least $25,000;
- Have lived in Liberia for at least ten years;
- The president may not be from the same county as the vice president.

Presidential Flag

Official Seal of Liberia

National Flag of Liberia - Lone Star

Office of the President

Before Liberia became a country, Africans in their different regions[1] were ruled by kings. When the settlers came to the region, their settlements were ruled by agents and later governors. The Office of the President was created in 1847 when Liberia gained her independence[2].

The President of the Republic of Liberia holds[3] the highest office in the nation. The President is the:
- Head of State
- Head of the Government
- The Commander in Chief of the National Army

After election, the President and the Vice President take a *solemn oath*[4] to preserve, protect and defend the Constitution[5] and laws of the Republic of Liberia, and faithfully do the duties of the Executive[6] office.

---

1 An area with no main boundary.
2 No longer under the control of another.
3 To have a position of being in charge.
4 A very serious promise to do something particular.
5 A set of written rules that our government Follows.
6 Carrying out the law and business of the country's affairs.

The Executive Mansion

The Executive Mansion is the official residence and workplace of the President. The current building was built during the presidency of William V. S. Tubman. The construction started in 1961, and was completed in 1964.

Joseph Jenkins Roberts

Born: March 15, 1809, Norfolk, Virginia, USA
Died: February 24, 1876, Monrovia, Liberia
County: Montserrado County
Political Party: True Liberian Party
Vice President: Stephen Allen Benson

1st and 7th President

Joseph Jenkins Roberts was our first president. He was the governor[1] of the Commonwealth of Liberia before becoming president. Under his leadership, the Republic of Liberia was founded on July 26, 1847 with three counties; Montserrado, Grand Bassa and Sinoe. He was also our 7th president.

---

1 A person who serves as an elected head of government. Like a president, he or she approve and enforce the laws passed.

Term & Time in office - 8 years 4 days
1st President: 1848 – 1856

Term & Time in Office - 4 years, 2 days
7th President: 1872 – 1876

Vice Presidents
1848 – 1850: Nathaniel Brander
1850 – 1854: Anthony D. Williams
1854 – 1856: Stephen Allen Benson

Old President's Mansion

National Holiday Day
March 15 - J.J. Roberts' Day
Honor Liberia's first president and his contributions to Liberia.

Fun Quiz

What was Roberts' job before becoming president?

Stephen Allen Benson

Born: March 1816, Cambridge, Maryland, USA
Died: January 24, 1865 Grand Bassa, Liberia
County: Grand Bassa County
Political Party: True Liberian Party
Term: 2nd President: 1856 – 1864
Time in Office - 7 years, 362 days
Vice Presidents:
1856 – 1860: Benjamin Y. Yates
1860 – 1864: Daniel B. Warner

2nd President

Benson became president in January 1856 and served for 8 years. During his term;
- Maryland became Liberia's fourth county on February 28, 1857.
- Napoleon III of France gave Liberia a container with military equipment for 1000 armed men.
- In 1862, Italy and the U.S. recognized Liberia's independence
- Liberia College was opened in 1863.

Fun Quiz

Businessman
Farmer
Preacher
Clerk
Storekeeper
Soldier
Judge
Deacon
Secretary
Vice President
President

President Benson did many jobs before he became president. Find them in the word search puzzle and circle them.

R	E	G	D	U	J	L	T	N	S	Q
B	N	L	Q	V	E	C	N	A	T	Y
J	K	J	M	C	V	S	E	M	O	R
N	K	Y	I	C	O	P	D	S	R	A
K	O	V	T	L	G	R	I	S	E	T
C	Y	C	D	R	E	G	S	E	K	E
N	L	I	A	M	Y	B	E	N	E	R
L	E	E	R	E	L	H	R	I	E	C
R	Z	A	R	C	D	W	P	S	P	E
C	F	N	M	K	G	Y	G	U	E	S
P	R	E	A	C	H	E	R	B	R	Y

Daniel Bashiel Warner

3rd President

Born: April 19, 1815, Baltimore, Maryland, USA
Died: November 30, 1880, Monrovia, Liberia
County: Montserrado County
Political Party: Republican Party
Term 3rd President: 1864 – 1868
Time in Office - 4 years, 2 days
Vice President: James M. Priest

Daniel B. Warner wrote our National Anthem in 1847, and the music was composed by Olmstead Luca in the early 1860s. He encouraged immigration of freed slaves to Liberia. In early 1865, the nation welcomed the first group of 346 settlers from Barbados.

Fun Quiz

Can you memorize our national anthem?

Liberia National Anthem
All Hail, Liberia, Hail!

Verse I

All hail, Liberia, hail! (All hail!)
All hail, Liberia, hail! (All hail!)
This glorious land of liberty,
Shall long be ours.

Though new her name,
Green be her fame,
And mighty be her powers,

In joy and gladness,
With our hearts united,
We'll shout the freedom,
Of a race benighted.
Long live Liberia, happy land!
A home of glorious liberty,
By God's command!

Verse II

All hail, Liberia, hail! (All hail!)
All hail, Liberia, hail! (All hail!)
In union strong success is sure.
We cannot fail!

With God above,
Our rights to prove,
We will o'er all prevail,

With heart and hand
Our country's cause defending,
We'll meet the foe
With valor unpretending.
Long live Liberia, happy land!
A home of glorious liberty,
By God's command!

James Spriggs Payne

Born: Dec. 15, 1819, Richmond, Virginia, USA
Died: January 31, 1882, Monrovia, Liberia
County: Montserrado County
Political Party: Republican Party
Term:
4th President: 1868 – 1870
8th President: 1876 – 1878

Vice President
1868 – 1870 Charles H. Harmon
Vice President:
1876 – 1878 S.J. Crayton

4th and 8th President

- He came with his family to the colony on March 21, 1829 on the ship Harriet.
- Payne was raised and educated in Liberia.
- He signed a peace treaty on March 1, 1876 between 9 Grebo chiefs representing the Grebo Kingdom, and the Republic of Liberia to have peace and equal rights to land ownership and trade[1].
- He became an Ordained[2] Minister in 1840
- He later received a Doctor of Divinity[3] degree from Liberia College in 1881.
- Spriggs Airfield in Monrovia is named in his honor.

---

1 Business of buying and selling items.
2 To make a person a Christian minister or priest by a special ceremony.
3 To study religion.

Term & Time in Office - 1 year, 362 days
4th President: 1868 – 1870

Term & Time in Office - 2 years, 4 days
8th President: 1876 – 1878

Back view of
James Spring Payne airport
in Sinkor, Monrovia.

10

Edward James Roye

Born: February 3, 1815, Newark, Ohio, USA
Died: February 11, 1872, Monrovia, Liberia
County: Montserrado County
Political Party: True Whig Party
Term 5th President: 1870 – 1871
Time in Office - 1 year, 296 days
Vice President: James Skivring Smith

5th President

Edward James Roye was born in Newark, Ohio in 1815. He was of pure African descent from the Ibo tribe of Nigeria. He attended the University of Athens, Ohio from 1832-1835, and Oberlin College between 1845 and 1846. After his wife died, he left Terre Haute, Indiana on May 1, 1846 and came to Liberia.

The Legislature[1] overthrew President Roye through a manifesto in October 1871. This was Liberia's first coup[2].

---
1 A group of people having the power to make and change laws.
2 A coup replaces a government's leaders.

Find President Roye's jobs in the word search puzzle and circle them.

Teacher
Barber
Merchant
Secretary of the Treasury
Associate Justice
Chief Justice
President
Speaker of the House
Journalist

Fun Quiz

```
W S E C I T S U J L C E
Q L E R F K L V W M S L
K J C C R E H M W U A R
T O Z R R H I D O S W R
N U B E T E C H S Y E T
E R Y H X D T O C B N R
D N G C H M C A R N K E
I A K A N I V A R B W A
S L R E A D B P R Y H S
E I L T V M Z X M P Q U
R S E M E R C H A N T R
P T M P R E K A E P S Y
```

11

James Skivring Smith

Born: February 26, 1825, Charleston, South Carolina, USA
Died: 1892, Buchanan, Grand Bassa, Liberia
County: Grand Bassa County
Political Party: Republican Party
Term & Time in Office - 67 days
6th President: 1871 – 1872

Vice President
October 26, 1871 – January 1, 1872
No One

6th President

- James S. Smith was born in Charleston, South Carolina in 1825. His family came to Liberia in 1833. Both of his parents died of malaria when he was very young.
- He studied medicine at the Berkshire Medical College in Massachusetts, U.S.A., where he received his medical degree in 1848.
- He served the remainder of E. J. Roye's term from November 4, 1871 to January 1, 1872.
- Smith was the first vice president to become president who was not elected.
- Dr. Smith served as the Superintendent[1] of Grand Bassa County for many years after his brief presidency.

1839 Storage Safe of the Ports of Edina & Bassa Cove

---
[1] A person who looks after or manages the county.

Anthony W. Gardner

Born: Jan. 24, 1820, Southampton County, Virginia, USA
Died: Early 1885, Monrovia, Liberia
County: Grand Bassa County
Political Party: True Whig Party
Term & Time in Office - 5 years, 13 days
9th President: 1878 – 1883
Vice President: Alfred F. Russell

9th President

- Anthony W. Gardner was born in Southampton County, Virginia, USA on Jan. 24, 1820.
- The family came to Liberia on January 11, 1831 on the brig Volador, and settled in Grand Bassa County.
- His mother died in 1865, but his father was still alive when he became president in 1878.
- Anthony W. Gardner received his education in the Liberian schools and later studied Law from the renowned Louis Sheridan.
- He was elected Sheriff of Grand Bassa County in 1844.
- Gardner was selected as a delegate representing Grand Bassa at the national convention of 1847, and was a signatory to the Declaration of Independence[1].
- He also established the Interior Department in 1880, Edward Wilmot Blyden served as the first Secretary of the Interior.
- Liberia joined the Universal Postal Union[2].
- Gardner resigned[3] on January 20, 1883 because he was sick. He was the nation's first president to resign.

---

1 The Declaration of Independence and Constitution were adopted on July 26, 1847, making Liberia, Africa's first independent nation and the world's 44th.

2 Universal Postal Union (UPU) is a part of the United Nations that organize and improve postal service throughout the world. Countries exchange mail, except parcel post between countries.

3 To give up a job or position by an official or formal letter.

Alfred F. Russell

Born: 1817, Lexington, Kentucky, USA
Died: April 4, 1884, Liberia
County: Montserrado County
Political Party: True Whig Party
Term & Time in Office - 352 days
10th President: 1883 – 1884
Vice President: No VP

10th President

- After three months travelling on the sea, the Russell family arrived in Liberia on July 11, 1833 on the brig Ajax which brought in a total of 146 settlers.
- The family settled in Clay-Ashland.
- Alfred F. Russell succeeded Anthony W. Gardner and served the rest of his term from January 20, 1883 to January 7, 1884.
- He was a Farmer.
- A Methodist Minister from 1837 - 1854.
- An Episcopal Priest.
- A School master in Greenville, Sinoe County.
- A Senator for Montserrado County from 1856 – 1860.

Boys Industrial dorm in Clay-Ashland.

Hilary R. W. Johnson

Born: June 1, 1837, Monrovia, Liberia
Died: February 28, 1901, Monrovia, Liberia
County: Montserrado County
Political Party: True Whig Party
Term & Time in Office - 7 years, 362 days
11th President: 1884 – 1892
Vice President: James W. Thompson

11th President

Fun Quiz

Find jobs President Johnson did before & after his presidency in the word search puzzle and circle them.

Secretary to President Benson
Principal - Day's Hope High School
Editor - Liberian Herald Newspaper
Principal - Preparatory Department at Liberia College
Secretary of State - 1865-1867
Professor of Philosophy - Liberia College
Postmaster General
Secretary of the Interior Representative in 1861
Coffee Farmer

```
K  R  R  S  L  T  D  W  L  Y
P  O  L  M  T  W  J  A  G  R
M  S  J  H  X  A  P  H  E  A
M  S  Q  K  N  I  T  F  N  T
V  E  M  M  C  R  A  E  E  E
H  F  J  N  J  R  H  X  R  R
J  O  I  R  M  R  G  K  A  C
J  R  D  E  T  P  R  W  L  E
P  P  R  E  D  I  T  O  R  S
P  O  S  T  M  A  S  T  E  R
```

- Hilary R. W. Johnson was born on June 1, 1837 in Monrovia, Liberia. He was the first president that was born on Liberian soil. His father was Elijah Johnson.
- Education at Liberia College
    - Master of Arts Degree in 1872
    - Doctor of Law Degree in 1882
    - He also studied music, and learned to play the piano, violin, flute and guitar.
- He was the Postmaster General[1] when W. D. Coleman was president.

---

[1] Someone who is in charge of our national post office. He or she is responsible to protect the mails.

Joseph J. Cheeseman

Born: March 7, 1843, Edina, Grand Bassa County, Liberia
Died: November 12, 1896, Monrovia, Liberia
County: Grand Bassa County
Political Party: True Whig Party
Term & Time in Office - 4 years, 313 days
12th President: 1892 – 1896
Vice President: William D. Coleman

12th President

Joseph James Cheeseman was born in Edina, Grand Bassa County when Liberia was still a colony. He was trained as a minister by his father, Baptist Missionary John H. Cheeseman, who died when he was 16 years old. He was ordained as pastor of the First Baptist Church in Edina in November 1868.

His administration focused on increasing the nation's revenues[1]. His administration bought a gunboat from Europe to patrol the shores and prevent steamers from entering Liberia's ports unauthorized. This controlled smuggling[2] of goods into the country and increased the national revenue.

His administration changed the nation's currency from paper note to gold.

---

1 Money collected by a government.
2 To take or bring secretly and unlawfully.

William D. Coleman

Born: July 18, 1842, Fayette County, Kentucky, USA
Died: July 12, 1908, Clay-Ashland, Liberia
County: Montserrado County
Political Party: True Whig Party
Term & Time in Office - 4 years, 29 days
13th President: 1896 – 1900
Vice President: Joseph J. Ross

13th President

William D. Coleman, his mother, and three other family members moved to Liberia in 1853. The family settled in Clay-Ashland.
- Coleman become President when Cheeseman died in 1896. He completed Cheeseman's term and was elected President two more times.
- With the help of Edward Wilmot Blyden, Liberia College was reopened to provide higher education.
- Annual payment of the 1871 loan began under his leadership.
- The nation's *bonded warehouse system*[1] was created at the six ports of entry where the Europeans traded. This allowed the government to control the flow of imports[2] and exports[3].
- He resigned on December 11, 1900.
- Vice President J.J. Ross had died and there was no VP at this time. The Legislature decided that Secretary of State, Garretson W. Gibson, should be president.

---
1 A government agreement or promise to do something.
2 To bring things (goods) into a country usually for selling.
3 Something that is sent to another country to be sold

Fun Quiz What is the job of the **Legislature**?

Garretson W. Gibson

Born: May 20, 1832, Maryland, USA
Died: April 26, 1910, Monrovia, Liberia
County: Montserrado County
Political Party: True Whig Party
Term & Time in Office - 3 years, 24 days
14th President: 1900 – 1904
Vice President: Joseph D. Summerville

14th President

Garretson Gibson was born on May 20, 1832 in Talbot County, Maryland, USA. The family, including his parents, Jacob and Rebecca Gibson, and siblings Joseph, Henry, Mary Ann, Samuel, James and Louisa, and their cousin Ellen Gibson, arrived in Cape Palmas on June 23, 1835.

When he became president, no one was Vice President at the time. He finished President Coleman's term and was elected as president from 1902 - 1904. Jobs before becoming president:
- Episcopal Priest
- Secretary of State[1]
- Chaplain[2] of the Senate
- Commissioner[3] of Education
- Professor[4]
- President of Liberia College

He was part of the delegation[5] to the US in 1908, along with VP J.J. Dossen, Charles B. Dunbar, Charles R. Branch and T.J.R. Faulkner. They met with US President Roosevelt and Secretary Taft to request aid[6] for Liberia.

---

1 A government official in charge of international/foreign affairs.
2 Religious official.
3 An official who is the head of a government department.
4 A teacher at a college or university.
5 One or more persons chosen to represent them.
6 To provide what is useful and necessary.

Arthur Barclay

Born: July 31, 1854, Bridgetown, Barbados, West Indies
Died: July 10, 1938, Monrovia, Liberia
County: Montserrado County
Political Party: True Whig Party
Term & Time in Office - 7 years, 362 days
15th President: 1904 – 1912
Vice Presidents:
1904 – 1908: Joseph D. Summerville
1908 – 1912: John J. Dossen

15th President

Arthur Barclay joined the settlers in Liberia in 1865 with his parents, Anthony and Sarah Barclay and his brothers and sisters. Arthur Barclay was raised and educated in Liberia. He studied Law and graduated from Liberia College in 1873.

Other Barclays who were well-known members of the government are Secretary of State, Ernest Barclay and President Edwin Barclay.

While he was president:
- The Liberian Frontier Police Force was formed.
- He made clear the nation's boundaries[1]
- Improved checking of the customs[2].
- The presidential term changed from 2 to 4 years. He was the first president to serve for four years.

Arthur Barclay was the last Liberian president born outside of Liberia.

---

1 something that points out or shows a dividing line.
2 tax (money) collected by the government paid on imports and outports.

Daniel E. Howard

Born: August 1, 1861, Buchanan, Grand Bassa County, Liberia
Died: July 9, 1935, Monrovia, Liberia
County: Grand Bassa County
Political Party: True Whig Party
Term & Time in Office - 8 years, 4 days
16th President: 1912 – 1920
Vice President: Samuel G. Harmon

16th President

Daniel Edward Howard was born in Buchanan, Grand Bassa County in 1861. His father, Thomas Howard, was Secretary of the Treasury. Daniel Howard was educated in Liberia at Liberia College where he studied Management.

He also studied under Edward Wilmot Blyden[1] who made his last visit to Liberia in 1912 to attend Howard's inauguration. He invited several influential native chiefs to his first inauguration ceremony.

While he was president:
- Liberia declared war on Germany on August 4, 1917
- German submarine bombed Monrovia on April 10, 1918, killing 4 people.
- Liberia was one of the signatories[2] to the Versailles Treaty signed on June 28, 1919 which brought an end to WWI (world war one).

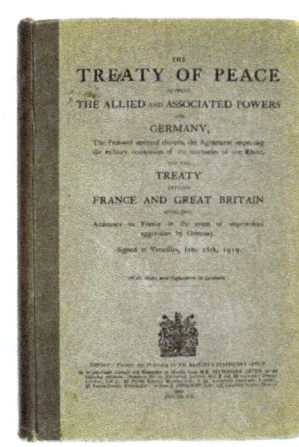
Treaty of Versailles

---

1 Edward Wilmot Blyden was a Liberian educator, writer, diplomat, and politician, who was born on August 3, 1832 in St. Thomas, Virgin Islands. He was known as the father of Pan-Africanism. Pan-Africanism is a belief that African people, those in Africa and those who live around the world, unify (come together as one). He died on February 7, 1912, in Freetown, Sierra Leone.

2 A party that has signed an agreement, especially a country that has signed a treaty (agreement betweet two or more countries).

Edward Wilmot Blyden

Charles D. B. King

17th President

Born: March 12, 1871, Monrovia, Liberia
Died: September 4, 1961, Monrovia, Liberia
County: Montserrado County
Political Party: True Whig Party
Term & Time in Office - 10 years, 332 days
17th President: 1920 – 1930
Vice President:
Allen Yancy

President Charles D. B. King of Liberia visits the Vatican in 1927

Charles Dunbar Burgess King was born in Monrovia, Liberia, in 1871. His father, T.O. King was a Nigerian who migrated to Liberia via Sierra Leone. He later earned his law degree from Liberia College.

Some of his jobs included:
- Liberian Ambassador to the United States
- Liberian Ambassador to the United Nations
- He represented Liberia at the Peace Conference and was a signatory to the Treaty of Versailles

While he was president:
- Liberia saw its first vehicle.
- The telephone system was introduced.
- In 1926 Firestone leased 1 million acres of land from the government and established the Firestone Rubber Plantation in Harbel.
- Was accused of forcefully sending native citizens to Fernando Po to work for free.

President King and his Vice President, Allen Yancy, resigned.

Many Liberian men that were taken to Fernando Po were returned to Liberia and their families.

Edwin J. Barclay

Born: January 5, 1882, Brewerville, Montserrado County, Liberia
Died: November 6, 1955, Liberia
County: Montserrado County
Political Party: True Whig Party
Term & Time in Office -13 years, 31 days
18th President: 1930 – 1944
Vice President: James Skivring Smith, Jr.

18th President

Eddie Barclay was born in Brewerville Township, Montserrado County on January 5, 1882. He was a professor, lawyer, poet, musician and politician. His most famous music is the Liberian patriotic song, The Lone Star Forever. Edwin Barclay was sworn in to complete King's term on December 3, 1930.

- Roberts International Airport was built in 1942.
- Open Door Policy[1] was started, and Tubman improve Liberia economy by encouraging foreign capital and business activities into the nation.
- US President, Franklin D. Roosevelt, visited Liberia in 1942. President Barclay visited the White House before he left office.

---

[1] The Open Door Policy was an economic action to create trade opportunities between Liberia and other countries to attract foreign investment.

Roberts International Airport was built in 1942. The US was given authority to operate and defend all air space and ports in Liberia. By 1843, the US Airforce and Army engineers began building roads into the Liberian hinterland.

William V. S. Tubman

Born: November 29, 1895, Harper, Maryland County, Liberia
Died: July 23, 1971, London, England
County: Maryland County
Political Party: True Whig Party
Term & Time in Office - 27 years, 201 days
19th President: 1944 – 1971
Vice Presidents:
1944 – 1952: Clarence Simpson
1952 – 1971: William R. Tolbert

19th President

William V.S. Tubman was born on November 29, 1895 in Harper, Maryland County. He was a lawyer before becoming president.

While he was president:
- Liberian natives were allowed to vote.
- Women could run for political offices.
- Established the public-school system.
- Some areas far from Monrovia became counties.
- The Executive Mansion, the Temple of Justice, and the Capitol Building were built.

Capitol Building

Executive Mansion

Temple of Justice

William R. Tolbert

Born: May 13, 1913, Bensonville, Montserrado County, Liberia
Died: April 12, 1980, Monrovia, Liberia
County: Montserrado County
Political Party: True Whig Party
Term & Time in Office - 8 years, 264 days
20th President: 1971 – 1980
Vice President: Bennie D. Warner

20th President

William Richard Tolbert was born in Bensonville in 1913. Tolbert was educated at Liberia College. He graduated in 1934.

Tolbert was a minister of the Gospel and at one time, served as pastor of Zion Praise Baptist Church in Bensonville. He was elected president of the Baptist World Alliance[1] in 1965.

When Tubman died in office in July 1971, Tolbert became the president since he was the Vice President.

While Tolbert was president:
- He raised the salaries of government employees.
- Stopped money every public employee had to give to the True Whig Party.
- He changed Bensonville name to Bentol.
- He changed the capitol city of Montserrado County from Monrovia to Bentol
- 1979 Liberia hosted the OAU[2] Conference.

President Tolbert was assassinated on April 12, 1980 in a military coup.

The nation continued under the leadership of the People's Redemption Council (members who took part in the coup, headed by Samuel K. Doe)

President Tolbert's slogans[3]:

"Mat to Mattress" and "Total Involvement for Higher Heights"

---

1 A worldwide group of Baptist churches agree to work together.

2 The Organization of African Unity is an organization to promote unity among African countries. Its name was officially changed to the AU (African Union in 2002).

3 Words used to attract attention to something.

Samuel K. Doe

Born: May 6, 1950, Tuzon, Grand Gedeh County, Liberia
Died: September 9, 1990, Monrovia, Liberia
County: Grand Gedeh County
Political Party: National Democratic Party of Liberia
Term & Time in Office - 10 years, 150 days
21th President: 1980 – 1990
Vice President: Harry Moniba

21st President

Samuel K. Doe was born in the town of Tuzon, Grand Gedeh County, and was from the Krahn tribe. He joined the Liberian Army at age 18 and graduated from the Tubman Military Academy in 1970. A year later, he earned a diploma from the Ministry of Defense Radio and Communications School in 1971.

After Tolbert's assassination, Doe headed the People's Redemption Council[1] and became the Head of State.

Liberia returned to civilian rule in 1985 and an election was held. Doe won the election and was sworn in as Liberia's 21st president in January 1986.

While Doe was president:
- He focused on promoting agriculture, encouraging people to grow their own food with the "Go back to the soil" campaign.
- The SKD stadium was built.
- The University of Liberia Fendall Campus was expanded.

---

1 A governmental body that was formed after the 1980 Liberian coup.

Samuel Kanyon Doe Sports Stadium

Charles Taylor and his rebels called "freedom fighters" started the second civil war on Dec 24, 1989.

Prince Johnson (INPFL) and his rebels assassinated President Doe on September 9, 1990.

Interim Leaders I

The civil war[1] in Liberia lasted from December 1989 to August 2003. During this time, many peace agreements were made, and a temporary government was organized to maintain order and security. The interim leaders were usually neutral parties not affiliated with any of the groups fighting.

---

1 A war between opposing groups of citizens of the same country

(1945 -)

An ECOWAS peace agreement was signed in Banjul. Amos Sawyer became the nation's interim leader in October 1990.

Amos Sawyer

President
Interim Government of National Unity of Liberia
Political Party: Liberian People's Party
Term: September 9, 1990 – March 7, 1994
Time in Office - 3 years, 179 days

(1935–2010)

David Kpomakpor

Chairman,
Council of State of Liberia
Political Party: Independent
Term: March 7, 1994 – September 1, 1995
Time in Office: 1 year, 178 days

(1937–2009)

Wilton G. S. Sankawulo

Chairman,
Chairman of the Council of State of Liberia
Political Party: Independent
Term: September 1, 1995 – September 3, 1996
Time in Office - 1 year, 2 days

(1939–2017)

Ruth Perry

Chairman,
Council of State of Liberia
Political Party: Independent
Term: September 1996 – August 1997
Time in Office - 333 days

Ruth Perry was selected as interim leader on August 18, 1996 in Abuja, Nigeria. She became the Chairman for the Council of State of the Liberian National Transitional Government on September 3, 1996. This made her Liberia's and Africa's first female head of state. She did not give in to the warlords[1], and refused all forms of temptation. Candidates[2] from 13 political parties participated in the elections held on July 19, 1997. Charles Taylor won the presidency.

---

1 A military leader
2 A person who is trying to be elected.

Charles Taylor

Born: January 28, 1948, Arthington, Montserrado County, Liberia
County: Montserrado County
Political Party: National Patriotic Party
Term & Time in Office - 6 years, 9 days
22nd President: 1997 – 2003
Vice Presidents:
1997 – 2000: Enoch Dogolea
2000 – 2003: Moses Blah

22nd President

Charles was born in 1948 in Arthington. He studied Economics at Bentley College in the US and graduated in 1977. While studying in America, he was a member of the Union of Liberian Associations in the Americas (ULAA) organization, and later became its chairman.

Taylor returned to Liberia in 1980 before the coup that removed Tolbert from office. He worked at the GSA while Doe was president. He was fired in May 1983 for embezzling[1] money from the Liberian Government. He returned to the US in October 1983.

On Christmas eve, December 24,1989, the NPFL and Charles Taylor, entered Liberia through Nimba County from the Ivory Coast. The civil war started on August 1990.

Throughout the war, ECOWAS and international organizations held peace talks with various warlords and signed many peace deals. But, most of these agreements were eventually broken.

Interim[2] governments were created from 1990 to 2003. Liberia finally held national elections on July 19, 1997. Liberians voted for Charles Taylor. Some were singing, "You kill my ma, you kill my pa. I will vote for you."

Charles Taylor was inaugurated as Liberia's 22nd president on August 2nd, 1997. He took over from interim leader Ruth Perry who was the first African female head of state.

About two years after Taylor became president, Liberia was again at war. the international community called for Taylor to resign and leave the country. Nigeria's

---

1 To steal money or property that you are put in charge of.
2 A period of time between events.

President, Olusegun Obasanjo, granted him asylum[3]. President Taylor resigned. He left Liberia on August 11, 2003 and went to Nigeria. Moses Blah was chosen to be Acting President.

---

3 Protection given to someone, especially political refugees

Interim Leaders II

(1947–2013)

Moses Blah

Acting President
Political Party: National Patriotic Party
Term: August 2003 – October 2003
Time in Office - 64 days

(1949–2014)

Gyude Bryant

Chairman
the Transitional Government of Liberia
Political Party: Liberian Action Party
Term: August 2003 – January 2006
Time in Office - 2 years, 94 days

Ellen Johnson Sirleaf

Born: October 29, 1938, Monrovia, Liberia
County: Montserrado County
Political Party: Unity Party
Term & Time in Office - 12 years, 6 days
23rd President: 2006 – 2018
Vice Presidents:
Joseph Boakai

Nobel Peace Prize

23rd President

After the end of the war in 2003, the nation was ruled by an Interim government headed by Gyude Bryant. Ellen Johnson Sirleaf won the next election on November 8th, 2005, defeating former football star, George Weah. She is Liberia's first democratically elected female president and Africa's first elected female head of state.

While Ellen Johnson Sirleaf was president:
- There was no war or uprisings[1] in Liberia.
- The government, businesses, and schools were open as normal.
- In 2010, she worked with the international community to forgive Liberia's national debt.[2]
- Several markets, bridges, and community colleges were built.
- New RIA terminal and Ministerial Complex were built.
- The hydroelectric plant in Monrovia was renovated.
- The Ebola crisis started in March 2014 and affected Guinea, Liberia and Sierra Leone.
- She ran for re-election in 2011 and won.
- She won the Nobel Peace Prize in 2011 and the Ibrahim Prize for African Leadership in 2018. She made many international appearances and speeches abroad.
- She was called the Iron Lady of Africa.

Roberts International Airport

---
1 An open fight by citizens against their government.
2 Money Liberia owe.

George Weah

Born: October 1, 1966, Monrovia, Liberia
County: Montserrado County
Political Party: Congress for Democratic Change
Term & Time in Office -
24th President: 2018 – Present
Vice President: Jewel Taylor

24th President

George Weah's family is Kru, from Grand Kru County.

- He dropped out of high school to become a professional[1] football player. He became a superstar and won many awards worldwide. He played football in Africa, Europe, and Asia.
- He is considered as one of the greatest football players of all times. He won Europe's best football player award, and FIFA World Player of the Year.
- George Weah went back to school after retiring[2] from football.
- In 1997, he served as a UNESCO[3] goodwill ambassador[4], promoting its immunization and HIV/AIDS prevention systems.

George Weah became a politician in 2004. He ran for president in 2005 but did not win. He became the senator for Montserrado County in 2014. Finally, in 2017 he ran for president and won.

He became Liberia's 24th president on January 22, 2018. He promised to fight against corruption and poverty in Liberia.

---

1 Taking part in an activity (as in a sport) in order to make money.
2 To give up a job for a long time.
3 United Nations Educational, Scientific, and Cultural Organization.
4 A person sent as the chief representative of his or her country.

Brigs & Ships

The Elizabeth was the first ship that took emigrants to Liberia. They left New York on February 6, 1820, for West Africa carrying 86 settlers. Find the names of many of the vessels used to carry emigrants in the puzzle.

Fun Quiz

Ajax
Alida
Atlanta
Baltimore
Banshee
Azor
Chatham
Elvira Owen
Estelle
Euphrasia
General Pierce
Globe
Golconda
Grecian
Harmony
Harriet
Hope
Liberia Packet
Madagascar
Mariposa
Mary Caroline Stevens
Mary Wilks
Morgan Dix
Oriole
Oswego
Perry
Ralph Ross
Regulus
Renown
Rhoderic Dhu
Rothschild
Royal Albert
Shirley
Sophia Walker
Spy
Strong
Vandalia
Volador
Zeno

```
N M A R I P O S A L W I L K S L M H Y R K
R H O D E R I C H M M X V O L A D O R O P
Z T A T L A N T A C K O T R H M F W C T A
G G K H A R R I E T G K R T L Y T X B H I
G A L R L V T W T L L M A G N W L A H S L
P I E R C E L Y A A O H A O A R V J Q C A
C S D D F B R W R L C W M R A N L A C H D
A A I W Q A A E K B K R E C Y M R F X I N
R R X M M V N L N C A E S N M T G A L L A
O H T R M E Y J T H W A R S M C R L L D V
L P L O G N P D P I G C M U B Z O J O P M
I U I Z G A S L D A M T F L A E S V Y B H
N E B A N I T X D H A O Z U N S S Q H O E
E S E L O C B A L D U G R G S T R H N J N
T N R A R E M Z I E S O M E H E Q E O W C
E E I Y T R O L M L H L Y R E L Z N O P T
K V A O S G A X K O I C B L E L N N N R E
C E B R E T R L G I R O C P N E E L E M C
A T T W J R W V Y R L N N T P R F B R B X
P S S O P H I A L O E D F B Z R L K L M X
Q O W E L V I R A X Y A F K M A P E R R Y
```

32

Liberia Presidents Crossword Puzzle

Write the last name of each president that matches the clues below.

Fun Quiz

ACROSS

5 Last Liberian president born outside of Liberia
8 Part of the delegation that met with US President Roosevelt
10 Studied under Edward Wilmot Blyden
12 Pure African descent from the Ibo tribe of Nigeria
13 Also the seventh president
14 Was also a medical doctor
18 Wrote the Liberian patriotic song, The Lone Star Forever
19 A signatory to the Declaration of Independence
21 The country's longest serving president
22 Changed the nation's currency from paper note to gold

DOWN

1 Represented Liberia at the Peace Conference after World War I
2 Wrote the National Anthem
3 Airfield in Monrovia is named in his honor
4 Father of our nation
6 Ex-wife is Weah's Vice President
7 Editor of the Liberian Herald Newspaper
9 Created warehouse system at six ports
11 Served as UNICEF Goodwill Ambassador
15 "Mat to Mattress" slogan
16 2011 Nobel Peace prize winner
17 Served twice as president
18 Opened Liberia College in 1863
20 First native Liberian president

The Declaration of Independence

A Declaration of Independence[1]
by the Representatives of the People of the Commonwealth of Liberia
in Convention Assembled on July 26, 1847.

---
1 Our constitution is a set of written rules that our government follows.

Written by Hilary Teage
Jacob W. Prout
Secretary of the Convention

Done in Convention, at Monrovia, in the county of Montserrado, by the unanimous consent of the people of the commonwealth of Liberia, this 26th day of July, in the Year 1847: In witness whereof we have hereto set our names.

Montserrado County
Samuel Benedict (President of the Convention)
John N. Lewis
Hilary Teage
Beverly R Wilson
Elijah Johnson[1]
John B. Gripon

Grand Bassa County
John Day
Anthony W. Gardiner[2]
Amos Herring
Ephraim Titler

County of Sinoe
Richard E. Murray

Fun Quiz

Find the names of all the men who took part at the convention.
Some names appear more than one time.
Circle each name in the puzzle.

T	N	P	F	Q	T	J	O	H	N	H	Y	N	Y
R	J	O	R	E	N	I	D	R	A	G	H	M	Q
E	O	Q	S	K	G	Y	L	R	E	V	E	B	Y
L	H	V	D	L	P	R	T	H	D	R	H	C	J
T	N	A	M	R	I	C	I	N	K	M	I	D	A
I	Y	L	O	U	I	W	F	P	I	R	L	B	C
T	Z	U	E	D	R	N	B	A	O	N	A	R	O
D	T	B	E	W	T	R	R	C	O	N	R	G	B
H	D	N	J	E	I	H	A	S	L	D	Y	N	H
S	E	L	A	H	P	S	N	Y	E	V	L	I	A
B	O	G	M	E	H	H	Y	N	U	C	X	R	J
W	E	M	H	J	O	H	N	N	M	J	T	R	I
Y	F	N	A	J	R	I	C	H	A	R	D	E	L
Y	N	O	H	T	N	A	K	G	S	R	R	H	E

---
1 Father of our 11th President
2 Our 9th President

The Lone Star Forever

By Edward J. Barclay

Verse 1
When Freedom raised her glowing form
On Montserrado's verdant height,
She set within the dome of night,
Midst lowering skies and thunderstorm,
The star of Liberty!
And seizing from the waking morn,
Its burnished shield of golden flame,
She lifted it in her proud name,
And roused a nation long forlorn,
To nobler destiny!

Chorus
The lone star forever,
The lone star forever!
O long may it float o'er land and o'er seas!
Desert it, no never!
Uphold it, forever!
O shout for the lone star's banner — all hail!

Verse 2
Then speeding in her course along
The broad Atlantic's golden strand,
She woke reverberant through the land
A nation's loud triumphant song,
The song of Liberty!
And o'er Liberia's alter fires
She raised the lone-starred flag unfurled
Proclaiming to an expectant world
The birth of Africa's sons and sires
The birth of Liberty

Verse 3
Then forward sons of freedom March
Defend the sacred heritage,
The nation call from age to age
Wherever it sounds 'neath heaven's arch
Wherever foes assail
Be ever ready to obey
'Gainst treason and rebellion's front
'Gainst foul aggression in the brunt
Of battle lay the hero's way
All hail Lone Star all hail!

Bibliography

Elwood D. Dunn, Amos J. Beyan, Carl Patrick Burrowes. 2000. Historical Dictionary of Liberia. Scarecrow Press.

Guannu, Joseph Saye. 1983. "Liberian History Up to 1847." In Liberian History Up to 1847, by Joseph Saye Guannu, 78. Monrovia.

Henries, A. Doris Banks. 1966. "Civics for Liberian Schools." In Civics for Liberian Schools, by A. Doris Banks Henries, 121. Collier-Macmillan International.

Henries, A. Doris Banks. 1963. "Presidents of the First African Republic." In Presidents of the First African Republic, by A. Doris Banks Henries, 102. Macmillan.

2021. History Of Liberia: A Time Line. https://www.loc.gov/collections/maps-of-liberia-1830-to-1870/articles-and-essays/history-of-liberia/.

n.d. Liberia: Past and Present. Accessed December 2020. http://www.liberiapastandpresent.org/.

n.d. Presidents of Liberia. Accessed 2021. https://en.wikipedia.org/wiki/President_of_Liberia.

n.d. Presidents of Liberia. Accessed December 2020. http://liberiainfo.co/prd/history/presidents/.

2021. Presidents Of Liberia Through History. https://www.worldatlas.com/articles/presidents-of-liberia-through-history.html.

Richardson, Nathaniel R. 1959. "Liberia's Past and Present." By Nathaniel R. Richardson, 348. Diplomatic Press and Publishing Company.

Liberia Literary Library

Liberia Literary Society

A global Literary Library for future generations.

The Liberia Literary Society library is a great place to explore literary works on Liberia and by Liberian authors. Liberia Literary Society has an online library, a database directory of every literary work by a Liberian author or work about Liberia.

For more information, please visit the websites:
www.liberialiterarysociety.org
www.library.liberialiterarysociety.org

Answers

S. A. Bendon's Jobs - Page 8

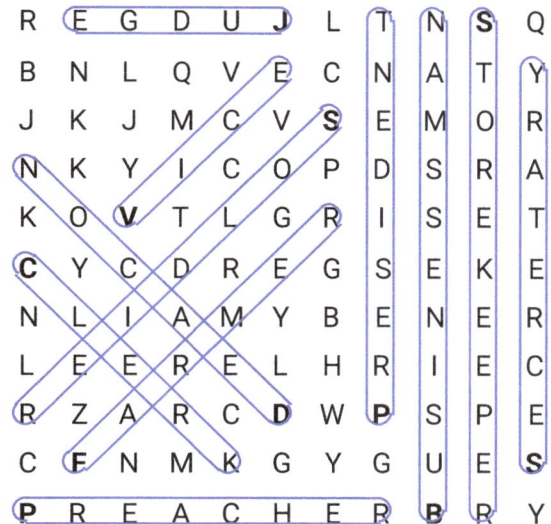

E. J. Roye's Jobs - Page 11

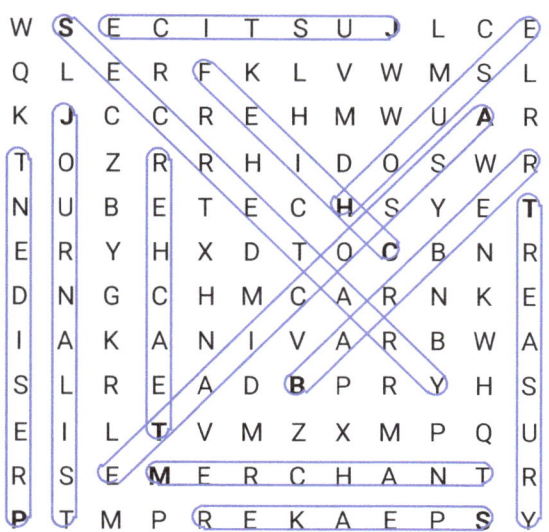

Hilary R. W. Johnson Jobs - Page 15

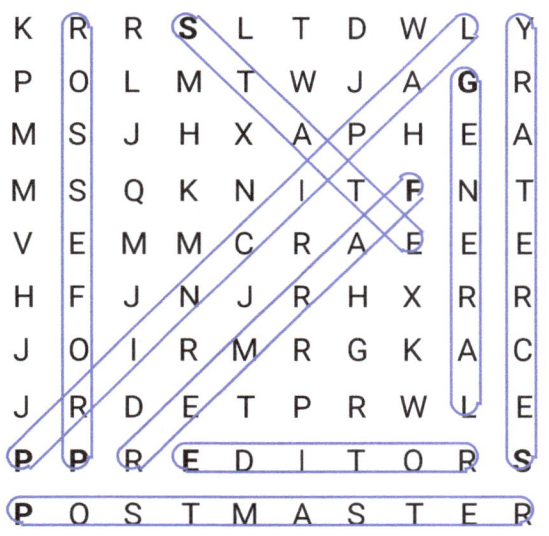

Convention Assembled - Page 34

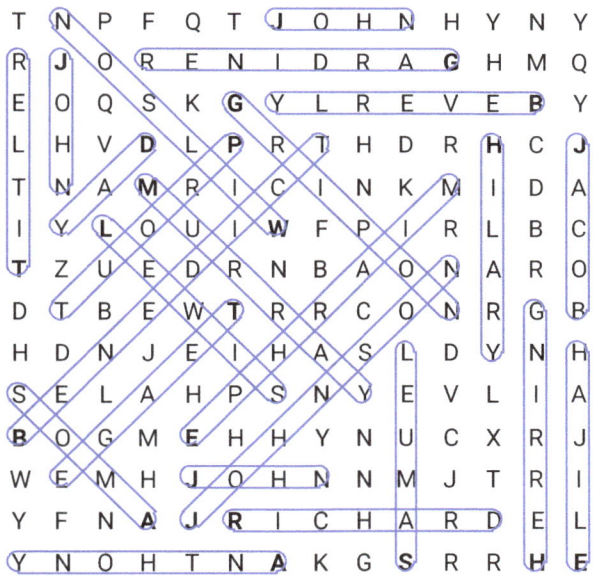

Liberia Presidents - Page 33

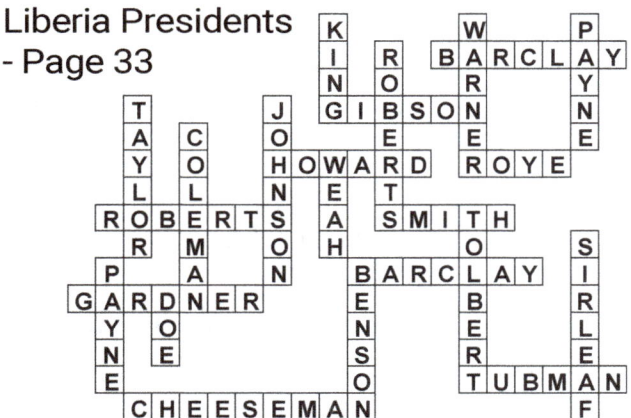

Briga & Ships - Page 32

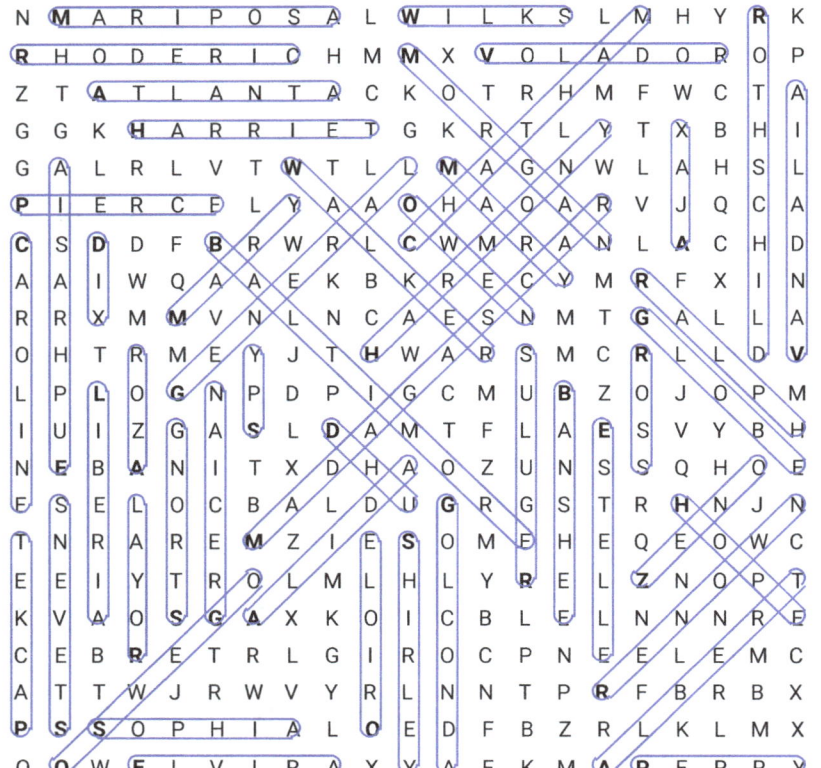

@ophie2020

Ophelia S. Lewis

Giving children a chance to learn is one of the most urgent priorities in Liberia. As a published author and humanitarian, Lewis takes on the dire yet fulfilling task of giving children an opportunity to start a solid educational journey. Quality education is key to any society's success; this ignites Lewis's passion for writing children's books.

Ophelia S. Lewis began writing children's books in 2009. A mission to transform the limited books available with African characters in children's books today, drawing from her childhood for inspiration, Lewis creates cultural-genre books with African characters all children can enjoy. Of her work, Lewis says, "The best way of getting people familiar with the importance of identity and own surroundings is through the eyes of childhood. Start at the earliest stage of life."

Lewis has created four children's book series: Reading Our World, Teacher Jeanette Kinder Kollege Workbook, Adventures at Camp Pootie-Cho, and Ian & Applecat. Joining the campaign to preserve Liberia's Sapo National Park in Sinoe County, Liberia, she created the series, Adventures at Camp Pootie-Cho, using native animals living in the park as characters people can easily fall in love with. She's joined by other authors who write for the series. Learn more about her work at www.ophelialewis.com.

www.ingramcontent.com/pod-product-compliance
Lightning Source LLC
Chambersburg PA
CBHW081759100526
44592CB00015B/2493